Entrepreneurship in Plain English

Farhad Haque

Available from Amazon.com and other retail outlets

Table of Contents

Introduction 4
Chapter One: Why become an entrepreneur? 7
    Risk of entrepreneurship 11
Chapter Two: Starting your own venture 15
    How to find ideas 17
    How to distinguish your business from others 26
Chapter Three: How to create your business plan 31
    Forms of organization of a business 31
    Writing a business plan 35
        Elements of a good business plan 37
Chapter Four: Setting up your business 48
    Various means of funding your business 48
    Choosing your business location 56
Chapter Five: Getting your first customers 65
Chapter Six: How to manage your finances 77
Chapter Six: How to be motivated while chasing a dream 85
Conclusion 90

Introduction

There is a current buzz about entrepreneurship; everyone seems to be talking about it. The recent advancements in technology which makes starting up a new business easier than it used to be contributed immensely to the high spate of entrepreneurs in the world now. But what is this entrepreneurship that everyone seems to be talking about?

In plain terms, entrepreneurship simply means the willingness to conceive, develop, organize and manage a business with all of its attendant risks. The most obvious example of entrepreneurship is the start of new ventures.

From the above definition, you see that entrepreneurship first has to start with an idea, this idea could be an entirely new one or an existing one that is simply improved upon. Next is the development of this idea, the organization of the idea, and finally the management of the business that this idea yields. In the definition, we saw that entrepreneurship comes with risks, and it is the entrepreneur who bears these risks.

The same way that entrepreneurship has risks, it also has benefits, especially when it is done right. And this aspect of doing it right is what we want to look at in this short guide. In truth, entrepreneurship can be scary because there is no guarantee that the idea will work, and the entrepreneur may end up losing money in the early years. However, if you read this book till the end, you will learn all about entrepreneurship and how to minimize its attendant risks. Without much ado, let started.

Chapter One: Why become an entrepreneur?

Before we go into details to talk about entrepreneurship, let's spare some time to talk about the benefits of entrepreneurship, why be an entrepreneur. Jumping this section will be like putting the cart before the horse. So, to motivate a lot of people who are still dragging their feet, let's quickly talk about the many benefits of being an entrepreneur.

1. Entrepreneurship offers you the chance of being your own boss

Many of us don't like working for other people, that's a fact. Even those who do work for others don't do it willingly. If you are among these people who like being in control of your time, then entrepreneurship is best for you. It offers you the chance to create your own business and manage it, so you don't answer to some other person.

With entrepreneurship, you choose who you work with and the kind of work you do. You also select the number of hours you work in a day or week. With entrepreneurship, you stand a higher chance of earning more significant income than people who work for others. However, without sugarcoating things, entrepreneurship has its risks, we'll get to see the risks later.

2. You are in control

Entrepreneurship offers you the opportunity to be involved in the creation of a business, development, and running of the business. It can be a thing of great joy to see your idea helping someone else somewhere.

3. It offers the prestige of being in charge

For many of us, the thought of controlling many employees and having many people answer to our call is a form of prestige, and that's what entrepreneurship bestows upon you.

4. It gives you the opportunity to build equity

Equity means selling shares of your company's stock to the public in return for money. You can pass down the equity of your company to your next generation, and that's a great legacy you have left for them.

5. Entrepreneurship creates an opportunity for you to contribute to your society

Look at some of the great entrepreneurs we have in the world today and how they have contributed to the society. Think of Mark Zuckerberg, think of Bill Gates. Through innovations of someone like Mark, you can stay in your bedroom and connect with your loved ones that you have lost contact with. With Bill's innovations that introduced the Windows Operating system, you can now make use of the computer even without knowing how to write computer codes.

You see, all of these people are contributing to their society, and they are not going to be forgotten even after they have left the world. With your entrepreneurial ventures, you can make contributions to your local economy; you can create an innovation that shakes the world.

Despite the above benefits of being an entrepreneur, we must not fail to understand that entrepreneurship is risky, but the risks can be minimized. And what are these risks of entrepreneurship?

Risk of entrepreneurship

1. Your venture can fail if you don't plan well

Yes, this is one of the major risks of entrepreneurship, your venture can fail earlier than you expected, leaving you with losses if you don't plan very well. It is a known fact that many new businesses fail within the first one year of its establishment due to lack of planning. Others fail within the first five years, and all of that happen due to lack of proper planning.

Now, if your venture or business fails, you bear all the risks, and that's why it is important that you research well before starting an entrepreneurial venture.

2. Raising startup costs may be daunting

To start a business, you need capital. Many times, raising this capital can be very challenging. Apart from your startup cost, you also need to have a lot of savings that can last you for up to six months or even one year because your business may not pick up immediately. Now, raising all the needed fund to start up your business is not often a walk in the park.

3. You may have to work longer hours

Even though entrepreneurship offers you the opportunity to choose when and how you work, you may still have to work longer hours than the person who is just working for someone else. For you to have your business up and running, you must put in extra time, more than the average number of hours that others put in.

4. No stable income

You may not have steady income especially in the early days of your business, and that can affect your personal life. Unlike the people who work for others and receive a fixed pay, your income will always fluctuate, and the amount of effort you put in will often determine how much you make.

5. You may lose the support of family and friends

Because of the long hours you have to work, you may not have a lot of time for your family and friends. And unless your family is very understanding, they may not support you. And that can affect you psychologically.

The above are just some of the few risks of entrepreneurship. However the risks, the advantages still outweigh the risks.

Having concluded this section, let's proceed to talk about how you can start your own entrepreneurial venture.

Chapter Two: Starting your own venture

As an entrepreneur who wishes to start up their own venture, you need to, first of all, come up with your own product or service idea. Without a good idea, you will find it difficult to make any meaningful impact. Your business idea is like the fuel that powers your car. Without the necessary fuel, your car won't be able to move. So, your business idea is what moves your business, and the success or failure of your business or venture depends on your business idea.

Every entrepreneur started their venture with an idea. Mark Zuckerberg, for instance, caught an idea which he developed to become the largest social media platform today. It all started in his dormitory;

he had wanted to create a system where people could rate pictures, and the idea escalated.

You can derive your business idea from an existing product or service, and you can also come up with an entirely new idea. If you see a need in your immediate environment that needs a solution with no one providing the required solution, that's an idea, and you can develop it.

Besides finding a problem that needs a solution, you can also come up with entirely new ideas, develop the ideas and go on to find a market for your product or service. Generally, many entrepreneurs find a problem in the society and develop a solution for the problem.

How to find ideas

There are many ways to find business ideas, and they include the following:

- Talk to people
- Observe your immediate environment
- Read books

By talking to people, you will be able to identify their needs that are currently not being met. You could also find out their needs that are being met but not adequately. For instance, if people have to visit the restaurant to get their food; a good idea could be to start a business where you help people to order food and deliver the foods to them at home. To know that people need this kind of service, you must have discussed with one or two people in a community.

So, if you are looking to start an entrepreneurial venture, go out there, talk to people, try to understand the problems they have that are not being met currently or that the solution is not adequate.

Besides asking people, you could also observe your immediate environment to observe the things that are lacking; then start a business that offers those things. The people who own Netflix looked at their environment and discovered that people had to walk down to the CD store to have their DVDs and they decided to develop a system that helps people to have their favorite films available to them anywhere they are provided there is an internet connection.

What about the developers of email service, they must have looked at their environment and saw that people had to wait for days, and sometimes weeks to have their mails delivered, and then they brainstormed and developed email system to solve the problem.

Another right way to get an idea for your entrepreneurial venture is through reading books. When you read books, you tend to understand the current happenings in your immediate community and the world at large. To be a successful entrepreneur, you must have a healthy reading habit.

When you are trying to get an idea using any of the above methods, the questions you should be asking yourself include the following:

- What current solutions exist, and what are the limitations with these existing solutions. For example, when those who developed email did so, there was a conventional method of sending mails through the post offices, etc. But they were able to improve the existing system and created a more efficient solution. So, when looking at your environment, ask yourself, *"what are the solutions that are currently available to the myriads of problems in the environment?"*

- Another question you should ask yourself when you are trying to catch an idea for an entrepreneurial venture is, *"would there be users of the new technology or solution?"* If you have observed your environment and discovered that people walked down to the restaurant to get their food. Ask yourself, *"Would these people want to patronize me if I create a service that helps them deliver their foods at home?"*

- Another question you should ask yourself is, *"do I have a way of improving products or services?"* Could it be that the existing product or service is too costly that the people are not able to afford it? Could it be that the existing product is not totally meeting the needs of the people? Could it be that the existing product is not readily available? When you answer these questions, you will be able to able to draw an idea from an existing product or service.

Your business idea need not be new per se; you can get an idea from an existing product or service, and then improve upon the current product or service to come up with something unique that addresses the problems of the people better.

Based on our explanations above, your business idea can fall into four categories. Let's look at these four categories below:

1. An existing good or service for an existing market

If your business idea falls into this category, you are going to do a lot of work to win over customers from the existing businesses. First, you would have to add an element of uniqueness to the existing products or services so that the existing market for the product can quickly switch over to your own product or service.

To float a business idea that falls into this category is usually more expensive because you have to spend a lot of money as initial capital to publicize your business and to add unique features to the existing products.

A perfect example of a business idea that falls into this category is Facebook. Before Facebook, there was MySpace, meaning that there was already an existing product doing what Facebook wanted to do. Furthermore, there was an existing market too. MySpace already had so many people who were using the service. Facebook simply needed to add special features and win over the existing users of MySpace.

2. A new product for a new market

Floating a business idea that is based on a new product for a new market can be quite challenging because you would have to put in a lot of effort to win over your first customers. To turn this kind of idea into a business requires a lot of research and careful planning; otherwise, the business would fail. One thing worthy of note is that if such a business succeeds, it has the potential to make you lots and lots of money.

However, these kinds of business ideas are usually rare, because almost any business idea you could think of today already has an existing product and market for it. Is it social media? There are already so many social media channels and users. Is it improved health products? There are already so many health products available in their respective markets. What you need to do basically is to find a good existing idea, improve upon it, make it unique and the uniqueness of the product will attract a percentage of the existing market to your idea.

3. A new good or service for an existing market

Elon Musk's electric cars fall into this category of business idea. Before Musk started making electric cars, there was already an existing market for cars, but he added something different. Other cars were running on fossil fuel, but Musk thought about a car that runs on electricity. Because of the unique features he added to his cars, he was able to break into an existing market.

4. An existing good or service for a new market

For these types of business ideas, there are already products services and an existing market, but you can create the same product and target an entirely new market. Example, if a service like Uber is not available in your home country, you could create a similar service and make it available for people in your home country. This way, you are recreating an existing product for a new market. Your country people become the new market for the product. Another example, if you create a service or business that helps deliver pizzas to people at home, your product is not new, but you have targeted a new market. And your new market are people who don't like going out to the restaurants to get their pizza or those who are too busy.

How to distinguish your business from others

No matter the category that your business idea falls into, there are already people who have similar ideas and existing businesses running on the idea. Does that mean you shouldn't go ahead and create your own business? The answer is no. What every entrepreneur does basically is to study a new product and improve upon it to create their own unique product and get their own market share.

Look around you, and you will find that what we just described above is the same thing that most of the major entrepreneurs in the world do. Before Uber came on board, there were local taxis that were taking people from one place to another, but Uber had to study the existing service and then added a distinguishing factor. And their distinguishing factor is the way they make it possible for riders to order a cab right from their bedroom. So, what are the different ways you could make your business idea unique?

1. Differentiation

By differentiation, you are trying to make your product or service different from that of your competitors. Example, if your competitors are already dominating the online scene, you could make it such that your product is only for offline purchase, that way, you would have succeeded in differentiating your product from others. Many other ways of adding uniqueness to your product include making it smaller, bigger, easier to use, etc.

When your product is unique, customers will be more than willing to even pay a higher price for it even though it is almost the same as that of the other people. Example, Yahoo mail was existing for many years before Google mail, but today, not a lot of people use Yahoo mail because Gmail came in and took over the market from them. Gmail made email account opening so easy that you could open an email account in seconds and that's their unique proposition.

2. Find a niche and specialize in it

What this means is that you should develop a product or render a service that cater to the needs of a subset of the society. This way, you won't have a lot of competition to deal with, and you will be able to satisfy the needs of your small customers as opposed to when you would be trying to attend to the needs of a larger market. Example of a niche service is LinkedIn. LinkedIn is a social media platform, but it is not your conventional social media platform, it is basically for job searches and other related services.

If you live in an area where changes in population characteristics occur often, then you could consider creating a niche product or service that attends to the unique needs of a subset of the population. Example, if you notice an influx of young men who are between the ages of 18 and 25 into your area, you could start a business that sells men's snickers only. Furthermore, if you live in a society where there is a large concentration of students, you could start an internet café to cater to the internet needs of the students. If you live in a place where there are a lot of fitness enthusiasts, you could create a fitness studio. All these are just examples of niche business ideas.

The two methods described above are mainly how to distinguish your business ideas from others. In this section of the eBook, you learned that entrepreneurship starts with an idea, and then the idea is developed into a business. In the next chapters, you will learn how to develop your idea into an actual business.

☐

Chapter Three: How to create your business plan

If you have succeeded in coming up with a business idea, the next step you need to take to turn your idea into a profitable business is to create a business plan. But before we talk about how to create a business plan, we want to look at the various forms of business organization.

Forms of organization of a business

By the "form of organization," we mean "how you want to run your business." There are basically three forms of organization of business – sole proprietorship, partnerships, and corporations.

Sole proprietorship

As a sole proprietor, you own your business, take care of the finances and bear all the risks and the profit of the business alone. Most entrepreneurs start and run their business in this form. You don't need to file legal documents to run your business as a sole proprietor, all you need do is to research about your product, open a shop or office if needed, do some registrations if applicable and start your business. The disadvantage of running your business this way is that your business assets and your personal assets are tied together. So, if you go into debts, your personal assets could be at risk of confiscation to settle your debts.

It is natural that you will start your business as a sole proprietor and then partner with others as the business grows. As said earlier, 70-80% of businesses are run as sole proprietorships.

Partnerships

In partnerships, you are sharing the cost, risk, and profits of running a business with some other person. The advantage is that you get to share the risks of the business with your partner. The disadvantage is that due to individual differences, there is the potential for disagreements. So, no matter how well you think you know your potential business partner, it is still better you don't enter into partnerships especially at the beginning phase of your entrepreneurial venture.

Corporations

If you plan to expand your business into a large-scale enterprise in the future, then you should work towards running it as a corporation. When you register your business as a corporation, it assumes a separate legal entity from you the owner. So, you can borrow money with the name of the business, the business can be sued as a legal entity, and the business can acquire and sell a property. Registering your business as a corporation is costly depending on your location, and as someone just starting, you may not have all the money needed to carry out the processes involved.

What is the best form of organization for an entrepreneur? When you are just starting your business, it is better you start off as a sole proprietor and then register a corporation later if you intend to expand your business into a large-scale enterprise.

Writing a business plan

To start your business, you need a business plan. Research shows that 90% of businesses fail within the first 5 to 10 years of operation because of lack of proper planning and management. Other available studies show that 10% of business owners write a business plan before starting their business. What this means is that businesses fail because the owners don't consider writing a business plan as an important part of running their business.

There are many important roles that a business plan plays in your business, and you are highly advised to have one before starting your business. No matter the size of your business, a business plan is very important.

A business plan could be likened to the architectural drawing of a house. If you want to build a new house, you must draw a house plan. You don't just acquire land and start building on it. First, you would meet with an architect, tell the architect the kind of house you want to build; the architect will draw a plan that details all the features you want in the house.

That said, the same way you need a house plan to start building a new house is the same way you need a business plan to start your new business. Your business plan need not contain many pages, even one or two pages is enough. Basically, you just need to write down your projections for three months, six months, one year, etc. Your plan has to detail what you want for your business and how you intend to get there.

Elements of a good business plan

Having seen the importance of having a business plan, let's quickly look at the things that you need to include in your business plan.

Remember that your business plan is a living document that you will often need when you want to make important business decisions such as reaching new markets, hiring staff, or entering partnerships.

So, you have to spend your time to write it, don't treat it like a high school assignment.

Below are the important sections that your business plan must contain

1. Executive summary

Just like the name implies, this section is usually the first part of your business plan, and it summarizes what your business is all about. Even though it usually appears on the first page of your business plan, many people choose to write it last.

2. Opportunity

Every business must have a need or a problem that it is solving. If you are running a local courier business, the problem you are solving is that of getting packages from one end of town to the other. Immediately after the executive summary section of your business plan comes the opportunity section where you have to outline the problems that your business is going to solve. Make sure you have researched well enough to ensure the problems you want to solve are pressing ones.

Another question that this section of your business plan answers is, *"who is your competition?"* All businesses have competitors, and you need to identify who your competitors are. It is not just enough to identify your competitors; you need to know how to surpass your competition. And the information on how you are doing to do so is contained in this section of your business plan.

What are you going to do differently, aren't your competitors doing those already? How are you going to convince the existing market of your competitors to try your products or services? All these are important questions, and you must answer them in this section of your business plan.

Do you know you can add more products or services to your existing ones after some period of operation? Many businesses usually start with a particular product or service and then add more as the business continue to progress. If there are products or services that you would likely add to your business in the future, this is the section of your business plan where you state them. If you are selling weight loss products, for instance, in the future, you could add coaching to your list of available services. With your coaching services, you train people who intend to start their weight loss products business.

3. Execution

This section of your business plan contains how you mean to turn your business idea into an actual business. There is a difference between having a business idea and turning the same idea into a real business. Many people have ideas in their heads, but not many are turning their ideas into businesses.

To turn your ideas into an actual business, you have to develop the idea into a business first, then develop plans on how to sell the idea to consumers, how you are going to operate the ensuing business, and how you are going to measure success.

Your plans on how to do all of the above should appear in the "execution" section of your business plan. Remember, no matter how great your idea sounds, if you don't have a way of marketing it to consumers, then it is just useless.

And when you kick off the business, how do you measure success? These are things that should be in your business plan. The way you measure success is going to be different from the way some other person measures success because, in the real sense of it, success is relative. So, if your own measure of success is when 100 people subscribe to your service in a day, then include it in your business plan. If it is when you sell ten products a day, it should appear in your business. The reason why you need to include all of this information in your business plan is that you will always go back to the plan to assess how your business is fairing and how to make necessary improvements.

4. Team and company

If you are hiring a team to work with you, then you need to describe your team in this section of your business plan. This particular section of your business plan, like the other sections, is vital because if you are going to pitch your business to investors for funding in the future, they (investors) would like to know the team behind your project or business.

Furthermore, this section should contain the legal structure you are using for yourself business. Another name for "legal structure" is "form of organization" of your business. Is your business a sole proprietorship, a partnership, or a corporation? This is the section where you have to describe all of that.

Other information that should appear in this section includes the location of your business and the history of the business especially if you're updating your existing business plan after some years of operation.

5. Financial plan

Your business plan is not complete if it doesn't capture the financial plans you have for your business. If you are not making money with your business, then it is safe to say that it is not a business but a charity.

How are you going to finance your business? Do you have the funds required to kick off your business? Are you borrowing money from family and friends to start your business? Are you taking a bank loan? All these are information that should be contained in this section of your business plan.

Furthermore, you need to describe the financial future you envisage for your business in this section too. How much do you expect to be turning in after three months, six months, one year, etc. and how are you going to ensure that your business turns in such amount? What are the things you are going to do to reach your financial projections in one year? If you want your business to be worth $10,000,000 after the first two years, how are you going to do that? All these are important things that should be captured in this section of your business plan.

6. Appendix

As the name implies, this section is for any additional information that you couldn't chip into any of the main sections of your business plan. You can also include product images and other sundry information in this section.

One important information that should probably appear in this section of your business plan is your exit strategy. What is your next plan in case your business fails? No matter how well you plan your business, some circumstances can still cause the business to fail. Example, you could fall sick and become unable to manage the business properly leading to its failure. Remember, no one can manage your business like you. Again, a natural disaster could set your business back causing it to fail.

Besides the failure of your business, you could decide to sell the business to an investor, and in that case, you need to define your exit strategy too. So, in determining your exit strategy, you have to do so in the light of the failure of the business and the event of you selling the business to some other person.

Are you going to start another business in the same line of the former one? Or are you going to start an entirely new business different from your former? Depending on the event, if you are selling your business, you could become one of the members of the board of the new business especially if you grew the business to become a giant enterprise before selling. And you could also start up a new venture entirely.

All these exit strategies are what you should include in your business plan. Remember, if you are ever going to pitch your business to investors for funding, the investors would want to see all the things we have described in above in your business plan. If you have them, you have higher chances of securing funding.

Having talked extensively about how to write your business plan, the next section of the eBook will be focused on how to do the actual running of your business.

☐

Chapter Four: Setting up your business

After you have gotten a business idea, written a well-researched business plan, the next step is to do the actual setting up of your business.

This is usually one of the main aspects of running a business. To set up your business, you need to source for funds, look for a business location, bring in your products or service, and then get to the actual running of your business. We'll look at each of these steps one after the other.

Various means of funding your business

Business funding is the major problem that tends to limit the potential of many entrepreneurs. It is not enough to have a good business idea; if you don't have a way of funding the idea, the idea is as good as useless. Ideas alone are not enough; you have to fund the idea. If it is through ideas alone, everyone would own a business, but when funding starts proving difficult, many would-be entrepreneurs drawback. That said, it is important to know various ways of funding your business, and we are going to look at these various methods shortly.

1. Personal savings

As an entrepreneur, the best means of funding your business idea is by the use of personal savings. When you are funding your business with your personal savings, you don't have to go through long processes to access the fund. Again, you won't be obligated to pay back the money, no payment of interests, and most importantly, you won't be required to transfer the ownership of your business.

Furthermore, if you already have some funds, it will be easier to convince an investor or a family member to support your business. They will see a sign of seriousness in you and offer to contribute to help you finance your business. So, before going ahead to set up your business, make sure you have up to 80% of the funds you need to kick off the business as personal savings.

2. Friends and family

Your family and friends are your second option when it comes to securing funds for the launching of your business. But before family and friends can support your business, they would want to see a sign of seriousness on your side. You need to have done you research well to convince them that you have a viable business idea. You also need to show them that you already have some fund and that you are only looking for extra fund to complete what you already have.

No matter your relationship with friends and family, they will not like to bear the full cost of funding your business. The money you take from family and friends must be treated as a loan that you pay back. The essence of treating the money as a loan is to ensure they don't start wielding unnecessary influence on your business because of the money they put down.

Furthermore, never agree to have family and friends be a part of the decision-making process of your business solely on the fact that they are providing you with money. If you are going to allow them be a part of the decision-making process, then make sure that they have the expertise to do so.

An advantage of using family and friends to compliment your startup capital is that you won't have to pay interest, neither will you be required to fill lengthy paperwork. A major disadvantage is that if your business fails and they lose their money, your good relationship with them could get severed.

3. Credit cards

If you have personal credit cards, you can use it to finance some aspects of your business setup. The things you could finance with your personal credit include purchasing of printers, personal computers, photocopiers or other business equipment. These items don't cost much; moreover, in some places, you can pay a little money for them upfront and balance your accounts later.

Note, you can't possibly use your personal credit cards to totally fund the startup of your business, but as said earlier, you can use it to fund the purchase of office equipment and pay for other little expenses. A major advantage of using a personal credit card is that you can use it to pay for items you can't afford outrightly. A major disadvantage is the high-interest rate charged on credit card balances if you don't pay off the balances after a month.

4. Banks

Banks can be another source of capital for the setup of your business. However, you should only use bank loans as a last resort to fund your business. You could get bank loans to expand your business when it is already booming, but using it to fund your initial startup is not advised.

Securing bank loans as a startup business can be quite challenging because banks rarely lend money to startup businesses unless you can prove to them beyond doubt that your idea is going to be successful. They may require that you pledge your assets as collateral for the loan, and as an entrepreneur, you may not have an asset to pledge to the bank. If you have money in your savings account with a bank, you can use that money as collateral to borrow money from the bank to finance your business.

A major disadvantage of using bank loans to finance your startup is the high-interest rate the bank will require from you. You might find it difficult to make a profit from your new venture because you would have to keep channeling your profits to paying off your bank loans and interests.

5. Venture investors

Venture investors are independent investors who fund startup ventures that have huge potentials for growth. Many entrepreneurs are increasingly using venture investors or capitalists to fund their startup. A major disadvantage of using venture capitalists is that they might insist on retaining part ownership in your business if they must fund it.

The best means of funding your startup venture remains the use of your personal savings. With your own savings, you know that the business belongs to you alone and that you retain the right to propel the business as you wish.

Having seen the major ways of funding your business, let's look at the next step in the process of starting a new business.

Choosing your business location

In the past, businesses were located solely offline, but in this age of technology, a business can be located both offline and online. With the help of the internet, online businesses can be run from anywhere. You can even be running your online business from the comfort of your bedroom. You can also combine the two models when running your business – offline and online.

Offline business

If your business is going to be run offline, then you need to do a lot of research before siting the business. If you site your business in a wrong location, it may lead to the end of the business. What are the factors you must consider when siting your business?

- Are your distributors or suppliers nearby? You don't want to be spending scarce resources on transporting your products from your suppliers, so you want a business location that is near the location of your suppliers. Again, if your distributors have to travel long distances to get your product, they may turn to your competitor who is nearby to get their supplies.

- Is it a known place for the service you are rendering or the product you are selling? If you sell snickers to young people, then you don't have any reason to locate your business in a community densely populated by seniors. If you offer commercial cleaning services, then you would want to locate your business near commercial areas of your town or city.

- How many people who live or work in the area are your target audience? If you bring your business to the doorstep of your target audience, they won't have any option than to patronize you. For example, if you are a professional administrative assistant, you would want to locate your business in an area where there are big corporations that could need the services of an administrative assistant.

- How many business in the area are complement yours? Example, a courier/delivery business could benefit from a grocery store or a health clinic.

- What is the cost of leasing in the area? Of course, you are supposed to know that you shouldn't spend the bulk of your startup capital on leasing a business place.

- Is it a growing business hub with many opportunities in the near future?

If you have an excellent business location, next, you need to fulfil all the requirements of leasing a business place and then kick off your business.

Online business

There is an increasing number of entrepreneurs today who are starting their businesses online where they don't need a physical office space. Yes, the ability to work solely on the internet is one of the many opportunities that technology brought to us. You can now run your business from the comfort of your bedroom.

Now, if your business is solely a home-based business that is facilitated over the internet, how do go about kicking off the business after you have secured your startup capital? A website is the answer! When your new business is solely based online, a website becomes your office.

Besides serving as the location of your business on the internet, your site is also a valuable branding and marketing tool at your disposal. So, even if your business is based offline, you still need a website to market your products or services, even though you might not be needing one at the early phase of the business.

Running your business solely online entails that you should have a strong online presence and your website and your social media channels can help you achieve that. Visitors will be coming to your website for various reasons, and you need to answer their many questions using your website and also sell your products or services to them.

How you go about the design of the website is totally up to. You could hire a professional to help settle that aspect of your business development, and you could walk the DIY (Do It Yourself) path. If you are cash-strapped, then the DIY path becomes your best bet.

Designing a website on your own is not as difficult as people make it seem. With a few videos on YouTube, you could learn how to set up a WordPress website. Whether you are designing the website yourself or hiring a professional to do it for you, you have to ensure that it is well designed before launching it.

If your site is poorly designed, you could easily lose out on thousands of dollars initially and ultimately lose even more in potential revenue that you could be making from a well-designed and functional website. Furthermore, you have to make sure you choose the right domain name for your website. Let the domain name you are choosing reflect your business name and let it be impressionable, memorable, and above all, simple to pronounce.

Set up social media channels

Another great marketing tool in this age is the social media. Whether your business is running solely offline, online, or both, you need to set up social media channels for it. Every day, billions of people around the world visit the different social media platforms to connect with friends. By establishing a strong presence on social media, you will be bringing your business closer to your customers where they hang out. If you ignore social media, it means you will be losing lots of potential income.

That said, go ahead and set up social media channels for your business. Don't leave any of the platforms behind. Make sure that your name is the same on each of the social media channels, and that the name, like your domain name, reflects the name of your business.

It is not just enough to have a presence on social media; you need to also be active on there. You need to be updating your channels frequently. Remember that different kinds of posts perform differently on each of the social media channels, so, learn the kinds of posts that perform well on each channel, so, you won't be chasing away customers instead of attracting them. Example, Instagram is for sharing beautiful photos, use it to share the beautiful photos of your products, with little write-ups to explain the photos. Longer posts will thrive better on Facebook, and not on Twitter, so, when on each platform, stick to the kind of posts that perform well on the platform.

Having talked extensively about how to fund your business and secure your business location, the next thing we want to talk about is how to get your first customers.

Chapter Five: Getting your first customers

So, you have been able to conceive an excellent business idea, you have done your research, developed your business plan, gotten your startup capital, set up your business location, gotten your products and services ready; and you are now waiting for the customers to start trooping in droves. Let's burst your bubble, it doesn't work that way. Listen to these words, *"customers will not come to you as a new business, you have to take your business to them."* They could start coming to patronize you on their own accord after you have made a name for yourself, but for this moment that you are just starting, you have to take your business to them. Even the big brands you hear of today started in a similar manner. The huge customer base they have today were built over time.

Without mincing words, getting the first customers is usually one of the most difficult aspects of starting and running an entrepreneurial venture. It is like the first step that a newborn baby takes after which the child starts taking more effortless steps. As said earlier, even the big brands you hear today once faced the challenge of getting their first customers, but they surmounted the challenge, and if they could do it, you too can, especially if you follow the tips below.

Create a huge buzz about your new business

The best way to attract your very first customers to your new business even before launching the business is to create an initial buzz about the business; do this both online and offline. Do this even before the formal launch date of your business. Don't expect to wave some magic wand and make customers appear to you; you have to work to bring them in.

You could create a buzz about your business both offline and online. This depends in part on the kind of business you run. If your business has both online and offline presence, then you can create a buzz about it both offline and online.

When you are trying to market your business offline, the tips below will help:

1. Have some customized notepads with your business name and contact information on it

You should budget part of your startup capital for marketing your business. Without marketing, no one will find your business, so, setting some of your capital for marketing is a very good idea.

Creating custom notepads is not expensive, there are many online printing companies that can design and print a notepad for as little as $1 per notepad. So, with a budget of $50, you could get as may notepads to distribute to your potential customers as possible.

You could be asking, *"Why don't I just print flyers instead of notepads?"* The answer is simple, people rarely keep flyers, once they have glanced through the content on the flyer once; they throw it into the trash can. But notepads last longer with people, they could use it to write, and it would remain with them for a longer period. Any time they pick up the notepad to write or anytime they see the notepad lying on their desk, they remember your business and want to patronize you.

Don't get creative with the notepads; you only need to write your business name and your contact information on the notepads, then go ahead to distribute to as many of your potential customers as possible. Pretty soon, they will start checking your business out.

This strategy of using notepads to market your business works like magic; it is a way of playing on the psyche of humans. When you help people (which you are doing by handing them notepads to write on), they appreciate the help rendered to them and would want to reciprocate the kind gesture. And the reciprocation could be in the form of checking out your business or referring your business to someone else. Your potential customers could say something like, "Hey! I heard there is this new fitness studio down the street; I think you should check them out."

How do you get customized notepads? Check online; there are many printing companies that now offer these services online. They help you design and print anything with your instructions and ship your printed stuff to your address. They have the most competitive rates in the industry. As said earlier, you could get customized notepads printed for as low as $1 when you are printing in bulk.

If you are running an audio studio for instance, after printing your notepads, head to a place where there is a large concentration of young people and distribute the notepads. Visit colleges, high schools, etc.

Because of your low reputation in your niche, some prospects may find it difficult trusting you. But then, you can offer special offers until you have gotten a lot of customers more than you can handle.

Print business cards

In addition to printing and distributing customized notepads, you can also create business cards and always go to everywhere with the cards. Business cards are cheaper to print, and you will continue to use them even after your business has taken a good shape.

Your business card should be as simple as possible. It should have your business name, your name as the owner of the business, and then your contact details. Don't get creative with it.

Get social

Besides creating a huge buzz about your business using the methods described above, try and jump on social media and make a lot of "noise" about your business there. Even before your launch date, create a lot of posts on social media talking about your business. Engage people on social media, and keep talking about your business until a lot of people start talking about it too. This method works for both online and offline businesses.

Apart from creating normal posts on social media, consider running paid ad campaigns to get more people to know about your business. The best online advertising methods are Google AdWords and Facebook Ads. These two are the best because they allow you to target people in a specific location. For example, you could run a Google AdWords or a Facebook Ads campaign targeting only people in California if your business is based there. That's not all; you could target the specific age group you would want to view your ads. If your business caters to the needs of young people between the ages of 18 and 30, then you can set up your ads so that only people within that age bracket can see it.

Setting up online ads will cost you money, and it is definitely worth it. For a budget of $100 on any of the platforms, you can receive a lot of leads than you can handle. In addition to running paid ads, you can advertise your new business on free classified ad sites like Craigslist, etc.

Besides using the above methods to advertise your business, consider word of mouth advertising. Word of mouth advertising remains one of the most viable means of getting information passed from one person to another. Speak to your friends and family and let them know you just started a business. Sometimes, family and friends turn out to be the first clients of some new businesses. So, let everybody around you be aware of the kind of business you are running. Furthermore, don't forget to solicit the help of those around you in helping you spread the word about your business; this way, you may even get your first clients without spending a dime.

Use special offers to entice and hook your first clients

Everyone loves freebies and special discounts, so, exploit this human weakness to attract your first clients. Devise a coupon code and let those who use the coupon get special rates on their first business with you. Your goal at the beginning shouldn't be to make much money but to attract customers first.

Once you have gotten your first clients through the special rates your offer, make sure the product you are selling is of top quality. If you are rendering a service, make sure the service is top notch. If you offer excellent services, the customers you got through offering special rates will be willing to stick around even after you have stopped your campaigns.

Important: let your customers know that you are offering them special rates and that it is for a specific period. The reason is that you don't want them to get used to the special rates and expect to continue to pay lower prices for your services forever.

The above are sure-fire ways of attracting your first customers. Next, we want to talk about something that is very important in business – how to manage your finances.

Chapter Six: How to manage your finances

It is no longer news that many new businesses fold up within the first five years of their creation. It is not also news that the primary reason why businesses fold up is mismanagement of finances. Not many new entrepreneurs know how to manage their finances effectively, and it is usually because they don't know how to separate the finances of their new business from their personal finances.

If an entrepreneur succeeds in learning how to manage their finances very well, then the chances of running their business aground become almost nonexistent. So, how do you manage your finances as a new entrepreneur? The tips below will be of great help:

1. **Separate your business finances from your personal finances**

Before starting any businesses, you are often advised to have enough money in savings that can last you up to six months or even one year. You are expected to take care of your personal expenses and pay bills using this saved money. Never should you try to take money from your budding business to take care of your personal expenses. If you do that, then you are already preparing your business for failure.

While you take care of your personal bills with your savings, reinvest the profits you make from your business into the business within this period that you are living on your savings. Stock more products that your customers are demanding that you don't have, invest in improving your skills if your business is a service-based one. Just reinvest the profit of your business instead of using it to pay your bills. All these apply to when your business is less than six months old.

As your business continues to grow, consider opening a business bank account so that you officially make your business a separate legal entity. In the US, opening a business bank account would require you to have registered your business as a corporation, gotten your EIN (Employer Identification Number) and other legal requirements. Just follow the procedures and open a business bank account for your business, it is an official way of separating your business finance from your personal finances.

2. Create a cash flow budget

A cash flow budget helps you to record your cash inflow and cash outflow. When you have a good way of recording those as mentioned above, it becomes easier for you to comfortably pay all your expenses without straining your income. It also becomes easier for you to know how much you are spending to run your business, how much that is coming in, and how much gain you are making as well how much you want to reinvest into your business.

Your cash flow budget needs to contain the following sections:

- **Revenue forecast** – your revenue forecast section should be divided into two. The first part is for revenue inflows and should contain your anticipated inflows such as payment for goods sold, payment for services rendered, and accounts receivables.

The second part of your revenue forecast is for your revenue outflow and is meant to contain the various ways money leave your business. Example, operating expenses, staff salary, etc. should appear in this section.

- A second section should contain your expected profit at the end of each month. Simply subtract your cash outflow from your cash inflow, and you get your profit for the month or week.

Make sure your cash outflow doesn't surpass your cash inflow. And that's why it is important that you keep the proper records. Once you notice that your cash outflow is getting bigger than your inflow, then it is time to minimize your running costs and do the things necessary to improve your cash flow.

3. Prioritize and spend wisely

Through your cash flow budget, you should be able to know if your business is running at a loss or a profit. If you subtract cash outflow from your cash inflow in a previous month and you discover that you have a deficit, then it is time to do something about your cash outflow.

First, try and reduce your operating costs, for instance, instead of hiring staff for one-off tasks, consider outsourcing to freelancers. Rather than spending so much on printing promotional materials, consider reducing the amount you spend on such materials as long as you are still able to get quality materials.

You just need to identify the things that are not very important and minimize the amount of money you spend on such things.

4. Don't extend credit yet

In business, the term extending credit to customers means giving out goods or rendering services to customers on credit for them to pay back later. If you start extending credit early enough in your business, then you are obviously preparing the business for failure. Even big businesses that have strong accounts receivable departments (departments meant to recover money extended to customers in the form of credit) find it difficult to recover their accounts, not to talk of a small business. So, when you are just starting your business, don't be in haste to start extending credit.

In conclusion, the above are sure-fire methods of managing your finances as an entrepreneur. As a recap, the methods are:

- Separate your personal finances from your personal finances
- Create a cash flow budge
- Prioritize and spend wisely
- Don't extend credit yet.

In the next section, you will learn how to stay motivated while chasing a dream.

Chapter Six: How to be motivated while chasing a dream

The term motivation was derived from a French word, "*mouvoir,*" which means: *to prompt, to move,* or *to stir*. Other names for motivation include "*taking action,*" "*being fired up,*" "*feeling the kick,*" "*being hungry for doing something,*" "*drive.*"

From the above definition, motivation is what you need when all odds seem to be against you. It is the fuel you need to continue to move your entrepreneurial vehicle. Every once in a while, you are going to get depressed as an entrepreneur. Things could go really wrong in your business, and you begin to consider quitting. At these times, what do you do?

You need to tap into your well of motivation and continue moving once again. Once you lose your motivation, quitting becomes your next line of action.

That being said, below are the techniques that can help you stay motivated while chasing a dream.

1. Stay away from toxic and negative people

If you are facing challenges in your business, it is better you stay away from negative people. They are going to try bringing you down to their level. Toxic people are always negative, and they never see meaning in anything. They feel bad about themselves and want to bring anybody who comes near them down to their level. As an entrepreneur wanting to stay motivated, stay away from these people. They can give you many reasons to quit pursuing your dreams if you keep having them around you. When you are facing challenges in your business, talk to people of like minds instead of seeking the opinion of toxic people. This takes us to technique number two.

2. Talk about your dreams with people of like minds

Build strong relationships with people who share your dreams. When you feel your motivation level is becoming low, then talk with these people about your dream. They will help you pick up your zeal once more. There is a popular saying that goes like this, *"iron sharpens iron."* If you want to stay motivated while chasing your dreams, it is just ideal that you talk about your dreams with people of like minds.

3. Always have the big picture in mind

Do you dream of building a world-class business? What is that big picture you have? Whatever it is, always have it in mind whenever you think you are losing your motivation. With the big picture in mind, you won't let your present situation to make you lose your motivation or abandon your dream.

4. Don't be afraid of failure

Fear of failure is capable of making you abandon your dream. This kind of fear is one that is common with entrepreneurs. Instead of being afraid of failure, ask yourself, *"What is the worst that could happen?"* when you ask yourself the above question, you push ahead knowing that you always a second option even if your first option fails.

5. Don't think about your failure

Dwelling on your failure is one way to abandon your dream. Instead of thinking about your failure, learn from them, and move one. We all make mistakes, but if you keep thinking about your past, you won't make progress.

Other ways of staying motivated while pursuing your dreams include the following:

- Celebrate small wins
- Divide tasks into small steps to avoid overwhelming yourself with too much workload
- Get yourself a mentor
- Get inspiration from others who have walked the talk but don't compare yourself with other

Conclusion

Hope you have learned a lot of fundamental principles of entrepreneurship in this book? The onus is now on you to take action and implement all that you have learned. It is not always about learning, but about doing.

Indeed entrepreneurship possesses enormous potentials to catapult you into the realms of financial freedom, but you must have a viable idea, develop the idea, and nurture the idea into a sustainable business to enjoy all the benefits of entrepreneurship. First, develop a business plan, seek funding for your business, choose a location, launch your business, attract your first customers, manage your finances, stay motivated, and pursue your dreams.

Cheers!

www.ingramcontent.com/pod-product-compliance
Lightning Source LLC
Chambersburg PA
CBHW020601220526
45463CB00006B/2402